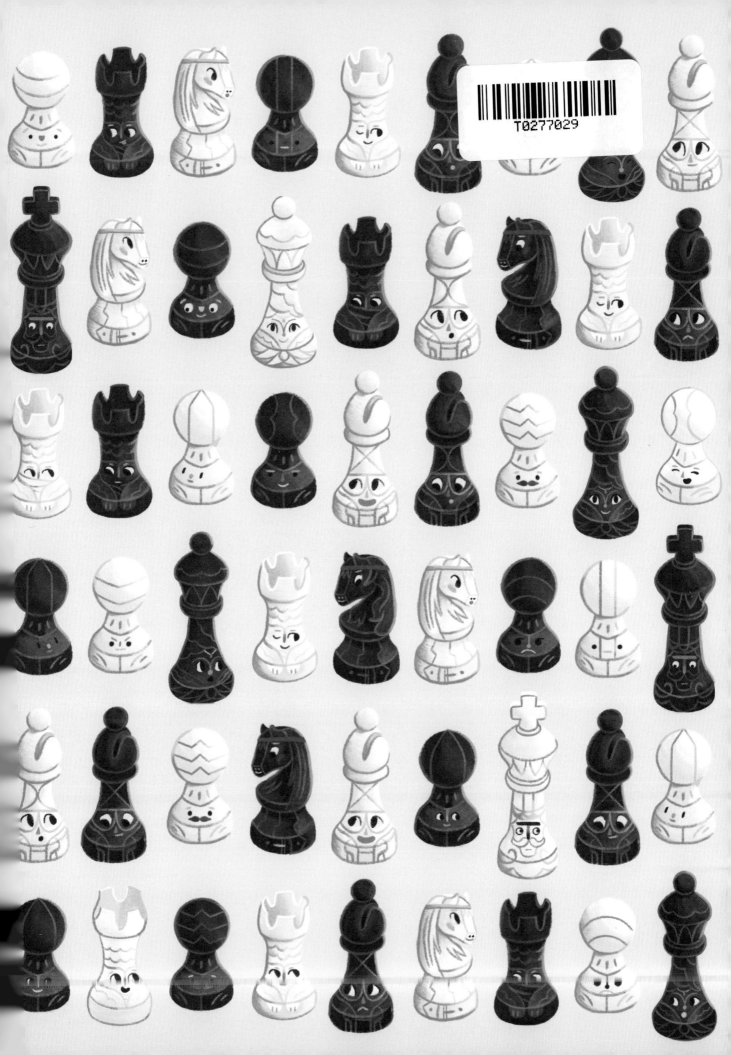

BECOME A
CHESS
CHAMPION

NEON SQUID

CONTENTS

WELCOME TO THE WORLD OF CHESS

Hello, future chess superstars! I am so glad you picked up this book. Starting with the basics, you will learn everything you need to play chess as a complete beginner. My goal is that by the end of the book you'll be winning games and hopefully beating some of your friends and family!

My name is James Canty III, and I am a professional chess player and coach on Twitch and YouTube. It is a pleasure to meet you! I am also a chess coach—I currently hold the chess title of FIDE Master and I'm working toward becoming a Grandmaster. Chess is my entire life!

In this book you will learn about the 16 chess pieces in this game and how to use them. The aim of the game is to checkmate your opponent, which means to trap their most important piece—the king. Along the way you will capture some of their other pieces and they will capture some of yours. It's a game of skill that requires intelligence, cunning, and bravery.

I've included some chess puzzles for you to solve throughout the book. They will help you become a better player. They're also fun! That's the most important thing—have a good time while you read this book and embark on your chess adventure. Everything else will come with time and practice. I can't wait to hear about your future success as a chess player—good luck. Let's go!

James Canty III

THE BOARD

Let's start with a quiz question: what is 8 x 8? If you said 64, great job math whizz! Chess is played on an 8x8 board, which means there are eight columns (called files) and eight rows (called ranks). Chessboards can come in different colors but they are usually black and white, and the 64 squares on the board make a checkered pattern. Each player has 16 pieces to start the game—not that many, right? Despite that, there are trillions and trillions of possibilities of how the game can play out! Whoever is playing as white always makes the first move.

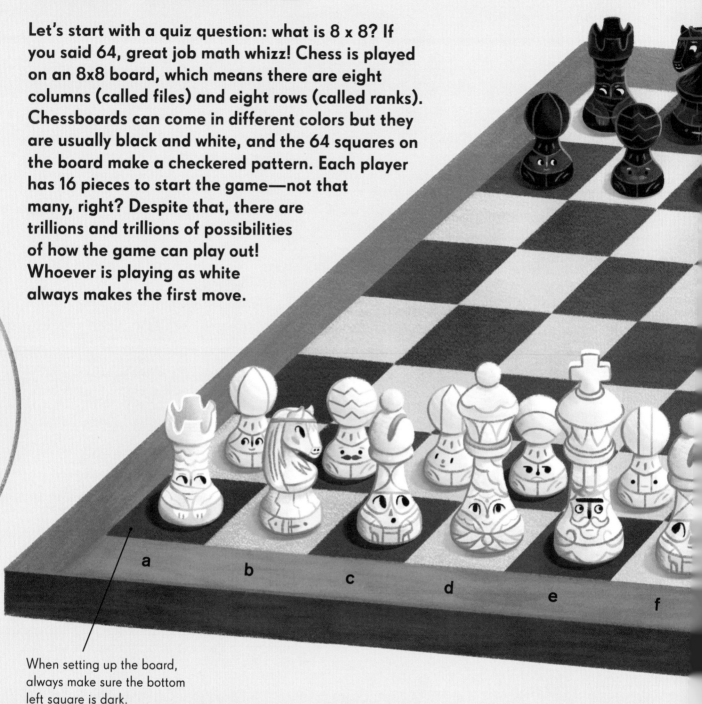

a   b   c   d   e   f

When setting up the board, always make sure the bottom left square is dark.

BEFORE YOU START, CHECK YOU'VE GOT:

8 pawns   2 bishops   2 knights   2 rooks   1 queen   1 king

Every file has a letter (a to h) and every rank has a number (1 to 8). The letters and numbers allow us to pinpoint any square on the board. For example, this rook is on h8.

8
7
6
5

HER MAJESTY IS ALWAYS HOME

Some white pieces start on dark squares and some black pieces start on light squares. The queen, however, always starts on her own color. The white queen goes on a light square (d1) and the black queen on a dark square (d8).

4
3
2
1

g   h

8 pawns   2 bishops   2 knights   2 rooks   1 queen   1 king

7

Meet the CHEEKY PAWN

Pawns are the starting point of almost every chess game. These little guys have a big impact! Think of them like soldiers who work together to help the rest of the army advance and defeat the enemy. Pawns are extremely valuable and how you use them determines how the game goes.

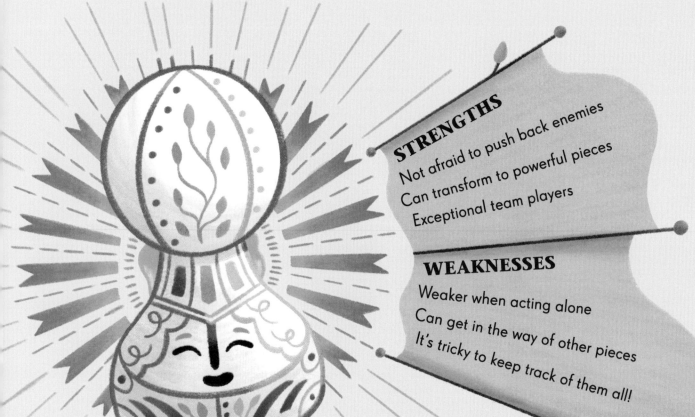

STRENGTHS

Not afraid to push back enemies
Can transform to powerful pieces
Exceptional team players

WEAKNESSES

Weaker when acting alone
Can get in the way of other pieces
It's tricky to keep track of them all!

SETTING UP

At the beginning of the game, each player has eight pawns. White pawns go in the second rank and black pawns go in the seventh rank. They should be standing in front of all your other pieces.

GETTING A MOVE ON

Pawns are usually the first pieces in the game to march forward! That is because most of your other pieces are stuck if you don't move these cheeky pawns out of the way. Pawns move forward until they are blocked by another piece, and they can't move again until the path is clear. They are slow movers, but sometimes slow and steady wins the race!

You can capture your opponent's pieces by moving one of your own pieces to a square currently occupied by one of their pieces.

In its first move of the game, a pawn can move either one or two squares forward.

After its first move, a pawn can only move forward one square at a time.

Pawns capture pieces by moving diagonally forward to either side and taking them. They can't capture pieces directly in front of them.

A pawn cannot move forward if another piece is blocking its path.

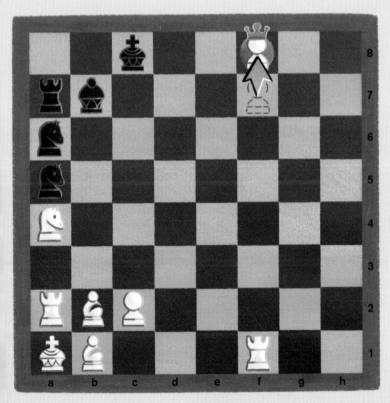

LEVEL UP

Pawns have a unique superpower: they can be promoted! When a pawn reaches the end of the board, it can be replaced by any other piece, except a king or another pawn. This is called pawn promotion. Players usually promote a pawn to a queen because it's the strongest piece. You could promote all of your pawns and end up with eight extra queens!

Meet the
JUMPING KNIGHT

Imagine you are minding your own business when all of a sudden a horse jumps over you! That's what happens to pieces on the chessboard when this pony is on the move. It may look and act like a horse, but this piece is actually called a knight. Let's find out more about it.

STRENGTHS

Can jump over pieces

Powerful in the center of the board

Has a wide range of movement

WEAKNESSES

Slower across the board

Weaker around the board edges

Can struggle to move around pawns

SETTING UP

At the beginning of the game, each player has two knights. If you're playing as white, place your knights on squares b1 and g1. If you're playing as black, your knights go on squares b8 and g8.

HOW IT MOVES

Knights don't let anyone stand in their way! When skipping, bouncing, and jumping all around the board, they move in the shape of an L. For example, they can move two squares up and one across or two squares across and one square up. This can be done in any direction, even backward.

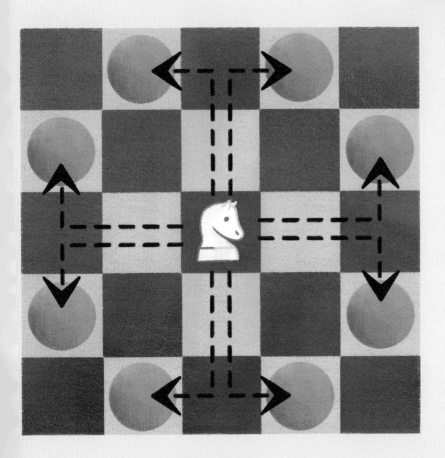

A knight is a bit like an **OCTOPUS** with its **eight arms**. It can jump to **eight different squares!**

Always try to keep your knights in the center of the board. The closer they get to the edges, the fewer squares they have access to, which means they're less powerful. Repeat after me: knights on the rim are grim!

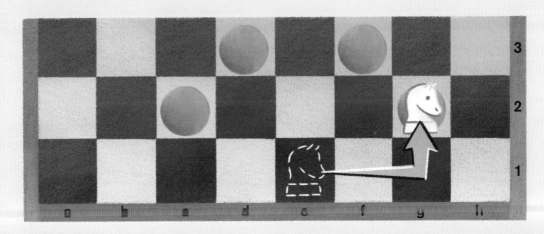

Meet the
SPEEDY BISHOP

Bishops are super-fast pieces, so if you blink you might just miss them! They are great over a long range, which means that they move all the way across the board. One moment a bishop can be chilling in the corner, and the next moment it can be taking a piece seven squares away from it. Speedy and sneaky—that's a useful combo!

STRENGTHS
Lightning-fast pieces

Can slide along the diagonals

Short- and long-range experts

WEAKNESSES
Can be blocked by pawns

Not very useful when surrounded

Weaker in the corners of the board

SETTING UP

At the beginning of the game, each player has two bishops. They sit between the knights and the king and queen. If you're playing as white, place your bishops on squares c1 and f1. If you're playing as black, they should go on squares c8 and f8.

HOW IT MOVES

Bishops rule the diagonals in a chess game. They can move diagonally in any direction, and if placed on the center of the board they can go in four different directions. There's one rule though: they must stay on the same-colored squares as the one that they started the game on. So if your bishop started on a dark square, it can only attack pieces that are also on dark squares.

DOUBLE TROUBLE

Having a "bishop pair," or both of your bishops, is always a good thing. If you have to choose between keeping both bishops or both knights, go for the bishops—this pair can cause some serious damage! If you have a "bishop pair" and your opponent doesn't, you can dominate the diagonals.

Meet the CLEVER ROOK

Rooks are strong pieces that never go down without a fight—no wonder they look like sturdy castles! Just like the bishops, these guys can move across the board very quickly. They also have a few tricks up their sleeves when it comes to protecting the king...

STRENGTHS

Super fast across the board

Biggest protectors of the king

Can threaten pieces far away

WEAKNESSES

Vulnerable if moved too early

Can get stuck behind pieces

Weaker when working alone

SETTING UP

At the beginning of the game, each player has two rooks. The rooks sit on the corners, on squares a1 and h1 for white and a8 and h8 for black. At first they're stuck, but they'll spring into action as soon as things open up!

HOW IT MOVES

Rooks are long-range pieces just like bishops, but they move in different directions. Rooks zoom around the board in straight lines—up, down, left, and right. When there is nothing standing in their way, they can surprise the enemy all the way across the board. When their path is clear they can move to 14 different squares! However, other pieces can easily block them.

ROYAL BODYGUARDS

While every chess piece has to defend the king, the rooks can use a special move called "castling" to keep him extra safe. They can swap places with the king in order to move him to the corners of the board and away from the firing line. Find out more on pages 44–45.

Stick with us, dude. We'll protect you.

Meet the MIGHTY QUEEN

All rise for the queen! The queen is the most powerful piece on the board. She does a wonderful job of protecting her king and attacking the enemy king. You only have one queen, so use her wisely and protect her carefully.

STRENGTHS

Can go (almost) everywhere

A master of quick checkmates

Can attack and defend well

WEAKNESSES

Can't jump over pieces

Vulnerable if moved too early

Usually the enemy's main target

SETTING UP

Can you guess where Her Majesty's throne is? If you said next to the king, bingo! This means that the white queen starts on d1 and the black queen starts on d8. They both sit on the square that matches their color.

HOW IT MOVES

The queen can move in every direction—up, down, left, right, and even diagonally. She can play like all pieces, except the knight. But don't let that power go to your head! Moving the queen out early usually exposes her to threats, so think carefully before you bring her into action.

Meet the
ANXIOUS KING

It's time to meet the man of the hour. Please give a round of applause for the king! The king is so important that every chess game revolves around him. The game ends when a player takes down their opponent's king. So whatever you do, make sure you move heaven and earth to protect this guy.

STRENGTHS

Can defend himself

Uses the rooks for protection

Strong at the end of games

WEAKNESSES

The slowest of slow movers

Vulnerable around multiple enemies

Needs protection from other pieces

SETTING UP

Each player has only one king. The white king starts the game on e1 (a dark square) and the black king starts the game on e8 (a light square). They sit next to their respective queens. This piece usually has a cross at the very top.

HOW IT MOVES

He might be a chess VIP, but goodness, he is a slow fella! He can only move one square at a time in any direction. The king becomes stronger toward the end of the game when there are fewer pieces on the board. When he's under threat and surrounded by lots of other pieces... that's when things get tricky!

Gulp! I would be in big trouble if it wasn't for my loyal army. Special shoutout to the rooks who can protect me by castling. See pages 44–45.

GAME OVER

The king can never be captured, but he can be checkmated. The game ends when the king is checkmated (see pages 26–27). It does not matter how or when, once checkmate happens there can be no more play. Until then, keep attacking your opponent's king and protecting your king against their attacks.

INDIAN BATTLES

In the 6th century CE, India was governed by the Gupta empire. When a prince was killed in battle, legend says his brother showed their grieving mother what had happened using a board and pieces. This turned into a game called chaturanga, which later became chess.

This would make a great game...

ANCIENT ORIGINS

The history of chess can be traced back to India nearly 1,500 years ago, making it the oldest board game in the world. Different legends from different parts of the world have tried to explain how chess was invented. Over time, lots of things have changed about the game. Early forms of the game didn't even have a queen, and epic matches could last several days!

CHINESE WARRIORS

Another legend says that in 200 BCE, Chinese commander Han Xin used pieces and a board to explain a plan for an upcoming battle to his soldiers. After the war, inspired by the Indian game chaturanga, the modern game of xiangqi (Chinese chess) was born.

VIKING FIST FIGHT

Chess quickly spread around the world. By the Middle Ages, the Vikings were playing it in Scandinavia, in northern Europe. Hnefatafl (Viking chess) was a popular medieval game played on a board much bigger than modern chessboards, sometimes measuring 13 squares long and 13 squares wide. Hnefatafl means "fist table"—they liked to fight it out on the board!

YOU'RE IN CHECK!

Hold on a second... What exactly does that mean? Being in check means that one of your opponent's pieces is threatening your king and could checkmate him with their next move. The player checking their opponent's king should say "check" out loud! Check isn't the same as checkmate, because you still have a chance to save your king, whereas checkmate always ends the game. The piece delivering a check could be a pawn, a knight, a bishop, a rook, or the queen. So apart from the opposing king, any piece can check the king. Let's see how they do it!

THE KNIGHT

Remember how these little ponies move in the shape of an L in any direction? That's also how they check the king.

THE PAWN

Even these little guys intimidate the king from time to time. They can put him in check diagonally, to the left or the right, if they are close enough.

THE BISHOP

Bishops can check the king from far away because they are long-range pieces. They can also check from up close, so keep your eyes peeled.

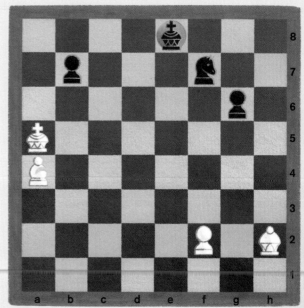

THE ROOK

Rooks love open lanes, so when there's nothing standing between them and the king they can put him in check.

THE QUEEN

The queen can check the king from any direction and any distance. When she checks, it usually means that the end of the game is near!

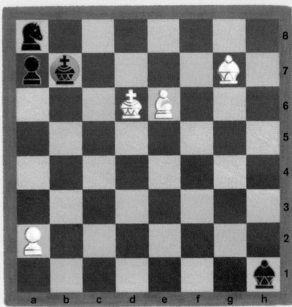

We're coming for you!

STAYING ALIVE

If you find your king in check, it's important not to panic and to keep thinking clearly. You need to act to save him. Luckily there are three different things you can do. You need to perform CPR: Capture, Protect, or Run away! Here's how each one works.

CAPTURE

The first thing you should ask is: Can I capture the piece checking me? If you can, it might be a good idea to do so. On this board, the black rook on g2 is checking the white king on g1. The king can simply capture the rook to stop being in check. Problem solved! However, it's important to remember that every game is unique, so this may not be the best move 100% of the time. Think ahead—you don't want to capture one piece only to be checkmated in the next move.

> Blocking a check and capturing a piece at the same time is like killing two birds with one stone!

PROTECT

If you can't or don't want to capture, then try to protect the king from the check. This means blocking the check with another piece that will sit between the king and the checking piece. In this example, the black bishop on b4 is checking the white king on e1. White can move their knight from b1 to d2 to block the check.

RUN AWAY

When all else fails, it's time to run! If you can't capture the checking piece and you can't protect your king by blocking the check, your last resort is to move your king to a safe square. In this example, white can move their king from g1 to h1 to escape the check from the bishop on c5.

CHECKMATE, I WIN

What happens if you're in check but there's nothing you can do to protect your king anymore? Bad news, my friend—that's checkmate, which means that the game is over! When you are in checkmate, you can't capture the piece checking your king, you can't protect your king by blocking, and you can't run away to a safe square without still being in check. There is nothing left to do but shake hands and say "good game."

TRAPPED IN THE CORNER

Can you spot the piece checking the black king in a8? Going once, going twice... You guessed it—the white bishop (d5). Your opponent can't capture, protect, or run away so this is checkmate. Let's take a closer look at why.

The black king can't stay in a8 because the bishop on d5 is checking it.

The black king can't escape to b8 because the knight could checkmate him.

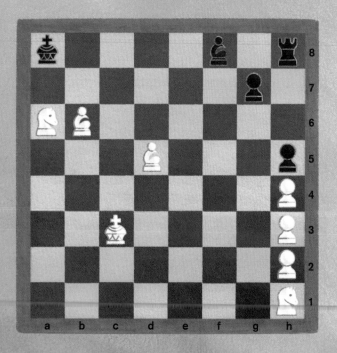

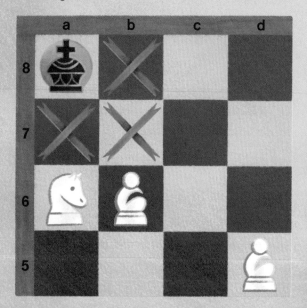

The black king can't escape to a7 because the white bishop on b6 could checkmate him.

The black king can't go to b7 because the bishop on d5 covers this square too.

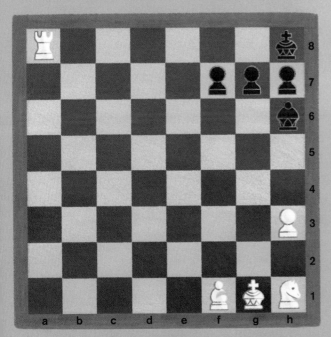

PAWNS IN THE WAY

The white rook on a8 is checking the black king on h8. Why is this checkmate? Let's think about it. Can a black piece capture the rook? Nope! Can black block the check with any piece? Nope! Can the black king move to a safe square? Nope! There is nothing black can do to get out of it.

The black king is in check so he can't stay on h8. He can't go to g8 because he would still be in check from the rook.

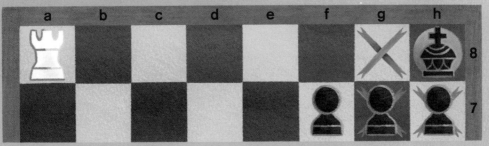

The black king can't run away to g7 or h7 because two pawns are blocking the way.

THE QUEEN STRIKES

In this checkmate, the queen on h5 is checking the king on e8, so he must move. The problem is, there is nowhere for him to go—so checkmate it is!

The black king can't escape to d8 because his queen is there. The bishop prevents him moving to f8.

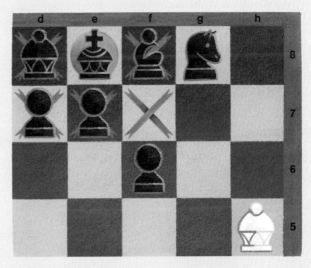

Pawns prevent the king from moving to d7 or e7.

The black king can't go to f7 because the white queen covers that square.

Solve the
PUZZLE

Now that you're familiar with the basic rules of the game,
it's time to practice! Here we have a chess puzzle. Solving
fun puzzles like this will help you improve very quickly—
try to do at least one a day!

 You're playing
with the white
pieces.

 Your opponent is
playing with the
black pieces.

 Mine!

Whose
turn is it?

STATUS OF THE GAME

Each player has exactly the same pieces: three
pawns, one rook, and a king. You can do a lot of
damage with just five pieces! It's black's turn to
move—let's see what they do.

Black moved their rook to e8, with a clear path to your rook
at e1. What should you do?

In my humble opinion, I think we should play it cool and make sure our rook is protecting our king.

I say we attack. Can we capture any pieces or put the black king in check?

The best move here is to capture the black rook on e8 with your rook. This also results in checkmate. I bet black wishes they hadn't made that move!

KNOW YOUR VALUE

Some pieces in chess are more powerful than others. A good way to remember this is by giving each piece a different value. Below, you can see how much each piece is worth. It's important to know the value of your pieces so you don't accidentally trade a queen for a pawn!

Pawn

Knight

Bishop

TRADING TIME

Sometimes in a match you can take an opponent's piece, knowing that they will take one of yours in return. This is called trading pieces. Ask yourself if the value of the piece you are going to capture is more, less, or the same as the one your opponent will capture. It's important you always get a fair trade!

A knight and a bishop are worth 3 points each, so this is a fair trade.

Two rooks (10 points) for a queen is not a fair trade because...

I'M PRICELESS!

Rook

Queen

King

The value of all the pieces on the board is known as the material count.

> 9

...the queen is only worth 9!

3 + 3 = 1 + 5

A knight and a bishop in exchange for a rook and a pawn is a fair trade because combined each pair is worth 6 points!

THE PAWN GAME

Before playing a proper chess match, it's a good idea to learn the basics and practice playing with different pieces. Let's start with the pawns! Your objective in this game is to get one of your pawns to the other side of your board before your opponent or to capture all of your opponent's pieces. I promise you—you'll learn a thing or two along the way!

SETTING UP

Your soldiers in this battle are the pawns. Just like in a normal chess game, white pawns start on the second rank, and black pawns start on the seventh rank.

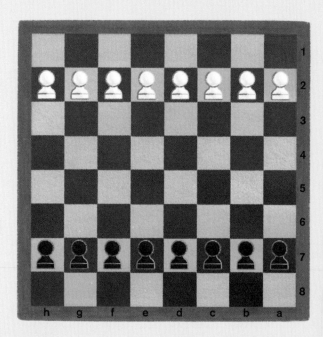

CHARGE!

Pawns always move forward, so keep them moving! You start the game with eight pawns for a reason—try using all of them. Remember they can move one or two squares forward if it's their first move, and one square forward at a time after that. If you need a refresher, go back to pages 8–9. Pawns can only capture pieces diagonally, so keep an eye on what your opponent is doing and be prepared to capture when you can. In this example, your black pawns on e5 and c5 can both capture the white pawn on d4.

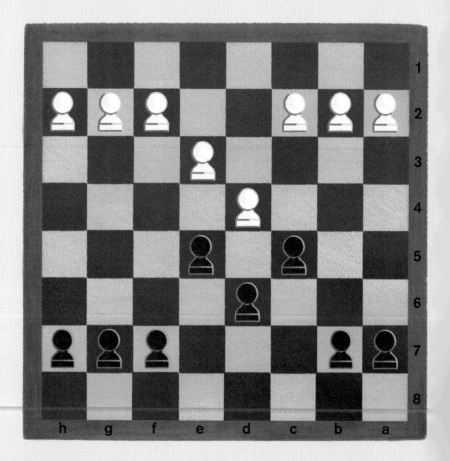

32

TEAMWORK

Pawns need to protect each other if they want to advance. A pawn protects another pawn by positioning itself one square diagonally behind it. This way, if your opponent captures your pawn you can claim revenge and take theirs! Here, your h5 pawn is in danger from the white pawn at g4, but by moving your pawn at g7 to g6 you can make sure you capture your opponent's pawn if they capture yours. It's tit for tat!

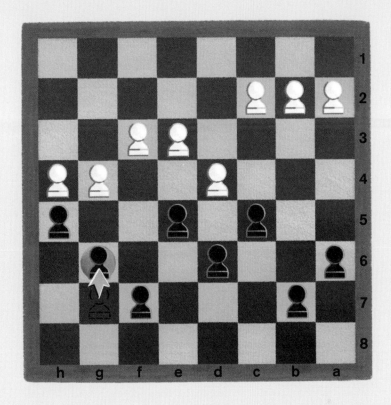

GAME OVER

A player wins the game if:

1) they capture all of their opponent's pieces
2) they reach the opposite side of the board...

...or 3) their opponent can't make a move because all of their pawns are blocked

THE KNIGHT GAME

Once you've won a few pawn games, it's time to take it to the next level and introduce the knights! The objective is still to get one of your pawns to the other side of the board before your opponent or take all of your opponent's pieces. But now you have your knights to help you out. Make sure to move both your pawns and knights as a team to win.

SETTING UP

The pawns are already in their starting positions from the pawn game so all we have to do is add the knights. White knights start on the b1 and g1 squares. Black knights start on the b8 and g8 squares.

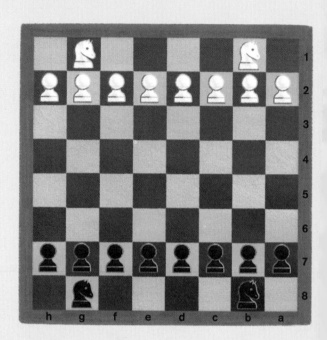

PROCEED WITH CAUTION

Use your knights to capture as many pawns as you can. Remember that knights capture anything that is an L shape away from them. The black knight on e4 could capture any of the pawns on c3, d2, or f6 on its next move. But watch out! When moving your knight, be careful not to place it on squares that are controlled by pawns. They can (and will!) capture your knights if given the chance.

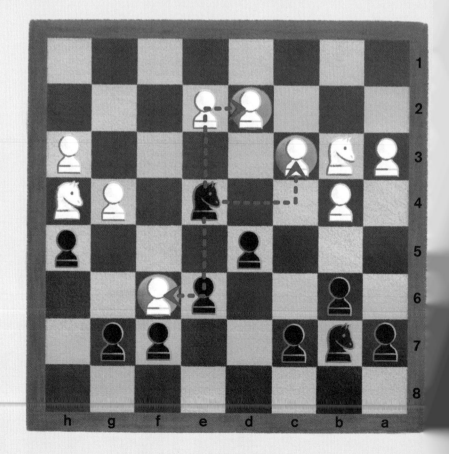

DOUBLE TROUBLE

One knight can threaten eight squares at once. Doing some quick math, how many squares can two knights cover together? That's right—up to 16 squares. What a magnificent duo!

WATCH YOUR BACK

Knights are sneaky because they can jump left and right, forward and backward! Sometimes it's easy to forget that all the pieces in chess (apart from pawns) can move backward. In this example, your knight just jumped back to capture a white pawn on f6. Result!

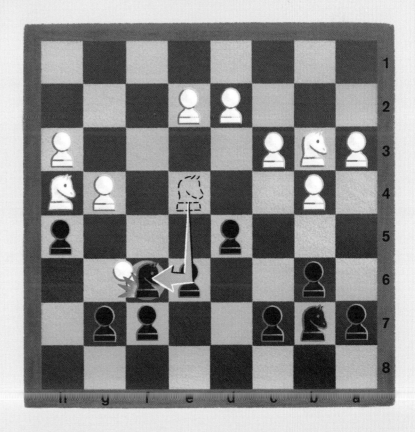

THE BISHOP GAME

Now that you're an expert on pawns and knights, it's time to add another piece. Enter the bishops! You're still trying to capture pieces and get one of your pawns to the other side of the board, but things are getting a bit more complicated now!

SETTING UP

With the pawns and knights in their starting positions, all we have to do is add the bishops. White bishops go on squares c1 and f1. Black bishops go on squares c8 and f8. You'll notice the board is looking more like a regular chessboard now!

TELESCOPIC VISION

Remember that bishops can attack pieces that are up close and far away. You might have a bishop tucked away in one corner while you're planning to use it to attack pieces that are all the way across the board. Your opponent won't see it coming!

PLAY TO YOUR STRENGTHS

In this game you have eight pawns, two knights, and two bishops, each with different strengths and weaknesses! Here, your black bishop on h7 (a long-range piece) is threatening the white pawn on c2. The pawn can't escape to c3 because your knight on b5 (a short-range piece) could capture it. That's what we call teamwork!

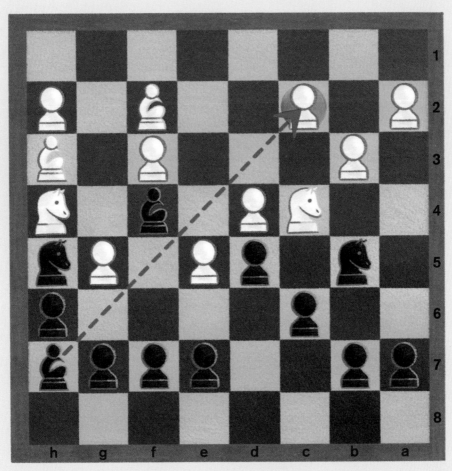

WATCH OUT!

Bishops and knights may be more powerful than pawns, but that doesn't mean you can let your guard down! Any piece can capture any other piece in chess. You don't want to lose a knight or a bishop to a humble pawn!

THE ROOK GAME

It's time to add even more pieces. Next in the lineup we have the rooks! These guys will really shake things up. With knights, bishops, and rooks now all on the board, it's going to be even harder to get a pawn to the other side or take all of your opponent's pieces. Are you up to the challenge?

SETTING UP

You know the drill by now, right? Pawns, knights, and bishops go on their starting squares. Place the white rooks on squares a1 and h1 and the black ones on squares a8 and h8.

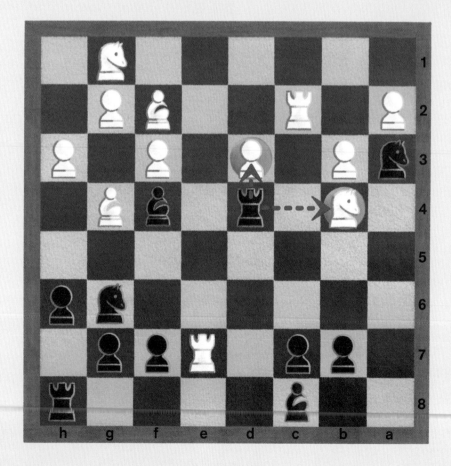

UP, DOWN, LEFT, AND RIGHT

Remember that rooks move in a straight line, capturing anything that's standing in their way. In this example, the black rook on d4 could take either the white pawn on d3 or the white knight on b4.

DO THE MATH

It's important to remember the value of the pieces you're trying to take. For instance, sacrificing one of your rooks to take a bishop and a knight from your opponent is a good trade!

Remember what you learned on pages 30–31 about the value of pieces.

POWER PLAY

Rooks are the most powerful piece we've met so far in this series of games. Use this power to your advantage and take as many pawns as possible, to slow down your opponent.

To add the queens to the game, remember that they go on their own color. The white queen goes on d1 (a light square) and the black queen goes on d8 (a dark square).

THE QUEEN GAME

It's time to add the most powerful piece in chess—her majesty the queen. The objectives of the game are the same as the previous games, but the queen's presence on the board gives you a few extra things to think about!

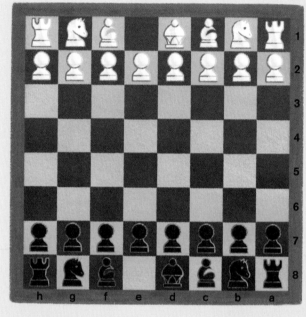

Can we have some help over here?!

SAVE THE BEST FOR LAST

You might be thinking, *awesome, I have the best piece in the game—now I'm unstoppable, hahaha,* but hold on a second. Firstly, your opponent also has a queen, and secondly, they will do anything they can to capture yours. Don't get your queen involved in the game too early—it would be disastrous to lose her.

PROTECT WHAT'S PRECIOUS

Be careful where you move your queen. Any of your opponent's pieces can capture her—even the pawns. Trading a queen for a queen is fine, but letting go of the queen in exchange for any other piece is a bad move.

If you sacrifice your queen, make sure you take your opponent's queen too!

WONDER WOMAN

The queen is like a bishop and a rook combined, meaning that she can take any piece diagonally (like a bishop) or up, down, left, and right (like a rook). The queen is very powerful but she's not invincible, and she can run into trouble if you're not paying attention. Here, she could capture the white rook on h2, the white bishop on e2, or the white knight on c3. However, capturing the bishop or the knight would be a mistake, because the queen would be putting herself at risk of being captured in the opponent's next move.

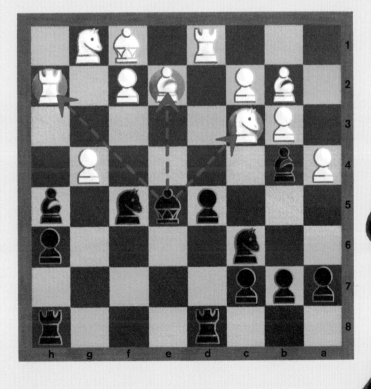

To play this game, place your pawns on their original starting squares on the second and seventh ranks from letters a–h. To add the kings, place the white one on square e1 and the black one on square e8.

THE KING GAME

Now that you're an expert on all the other pieces, it's time to focus on the king! Here your objective is still to get a pawn to the other side or capture all your opponent's pawns, but this time you can also win by checkmating your opponent's king!

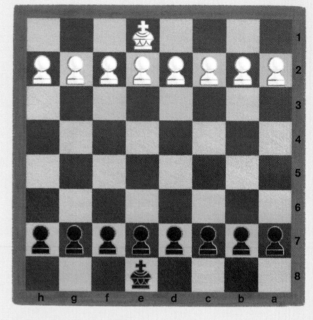

SLOW AND STEADY

In this game all pieces are slow movers—kings and pawns can only advance one square at a time. It might take a while for you to check or capture, but keep going. In this game, slow and steady can win the race!

SMALL BUT MIGHTY

In chess every piece can check the king, except for the other king. The same is true for this game. Remember that pawns are stronger when they work together. For example, here the black pawn at c4 is checking the white king at d3. If it was by itself, the white king could capture it, but as the black pawn is protected by its buddies at b5 and d5, the king has to come up with another plan to escape!

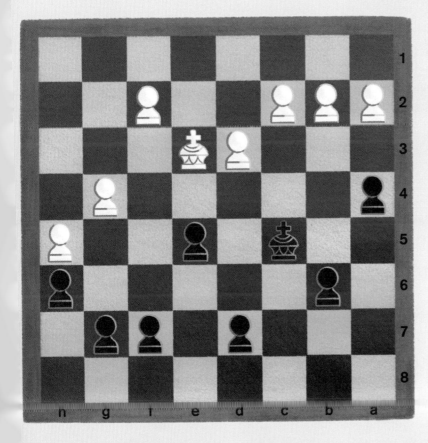

SHARING THE LOAD

No single piece should carry the burden of winning all by itself. Although the objective is to get a pawn to the other side, don't forget about the king! The king is the most powerful piece in this game, so make sure to use him. The king can be used to capture your opponent's pawns, block them from reaching the other side, and even help get your own pawns to the far end of the board.

CASTLING

KINGSIDE CASTLING

Castling on the kingside means doing this move on the king's side of the board—the right side if you're white or the left side if you're black. You can only castle when there are no pieces standing between the rook and the king, so you need to move your knight and bishop out of the way first. When castling on the kingside as black, in one move you can move your king two spaces across (from e8 to g8) and your rook to the other side of the king (from h8 to f8).

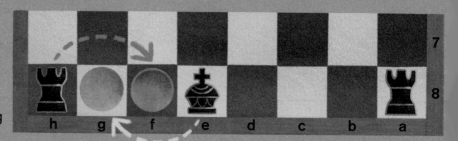

By moving your king to the far left of the board you can protect it from threats coming from the right.

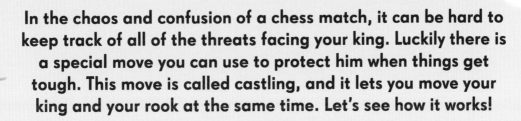

In the chaos and confusion of a chess match, it can be hard to keep track of all of the threats facing your king. Luckily there is a special move you can use to protect him when things get tough. This move is called castling, and it lets you move your king and your rook at the same time. Let's see how it works!

QUEENSIDE CASTLING

Castling on the queenside is similar, but you're switching around the pieces on the queen's side of the board—the right side if you're black or the left side if you're white. To do it, you first have to move the queen, the bishop, and the knight out of the way. Then the black king goes from e8 to c8 and the rook from a8 to d8. Whether you castle kingside or queenside, you move the king over two squares and put the rook on the other side of it.

You don't have to use this move, but in certain situations it is very handy! Castling is also a good way of getting your rook out of the corner so it can be more involved in the game.

45

Solve the
PUZZLE

When trying to solve any chess puzzle, always start by
scanning the board and asking yourself some questions:
What can I capture? Can I check my opponent's king?
What is my opponent trying to do?

You're playing
with the white
pieces.

Your opponent is
playing with the
black pieces.

Mine!

Whose
turn is it?

STATUS OF THE GAME

Both players have plenty of pieces on the board, which means
there are lots of opportunities to attack. Black has castled their
king, but there are still opportunities to break through their
defense. Can you find a way to checkmate?

Need a
refresher on
castling? Turn
back to pages
44–45.

Can we set a
trap for the
black king?

Black moves their queen from d8 to e7. This innocent-looking move leads to black's demise. What move do you think you should make?

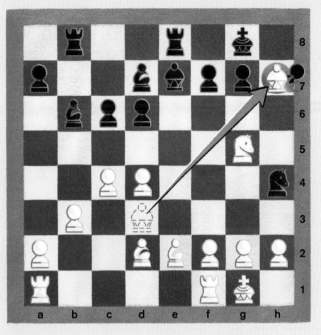

Did you say move your queen from d3 to h7? If so, nice one! Your queen takes the pawn and checks the king. Your knight is protecting your queen, so black will have to run away.

Black retreats their king from g8 to f8. They think they're safe, but are they? What's your next move?

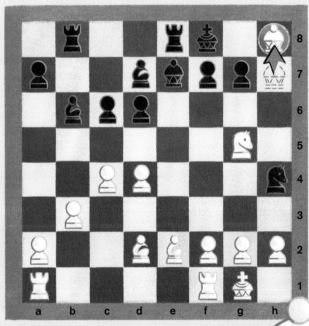

Hopefully you moved your queen to h8—that's checkmate! Black can't capture your queen, block the check, or run away. Good game!

THE BEST PLAYERS

Chess has been around for a long time. There are chess legends, prodigies, World Champions, challengers, amateurs, Masters, and Grandmasters. Guess who else is now part of this amazing club? You, of course! Unfortunately, we didn't have space to include you in this book, so that'll have to wait for the next edition. In the meantime, let's meet some of the greatest chess players of all time.

WILHELM STEINITZ

Wilhelm Steinitz (1836–1900) became the first World Chess Champion in 1886. He dominated the world of chess long before being crowned champion—he didn't lose a match for more than 30 years! Wilhelm also wrote a book with 432 different chess games in it and helped figure out the chess rules we use today.

EMANUEL LASKER

Emanuel Lasker (1868–1941) became the second World Chess Champion in 1894 and held this title for 27 years! He was an all-rounder—good at every aspect of chess. He also published loads of books, including six books about chess. Hear that, Wilhelm?

XIE JUN

Xie Jun (born 1970) started playing chess at the age of ten and became the Women's World Chess Champion at the age of 20, in 1991. She is a national hero in China for two reasons: she was the first Asian player to win this prestigious title, and her victory meant that the Russians lost their 41-year winning streak!

CHECKS, CAPTURES, AND THREATS

A chess game can be overwhelming at times, but in the heat of battle there are strategies you can use to make sure you make the right decisions. Before each move you make, you should first remember to look for three things: checks, captures, and threats.

CHECKS

The first thing you need to do is check for checks! Quick recap: check is when a king is at risk of being checkmated by the opponent with their next move. On this board, the white bishop on b5 is checking the black king on e8. Black needs to either capture the white bishop, protect their king by blocking the check, or run away from the check by moving their king to a safe square (see pages 24–25). Always be on the lookout for any checks you can make and any checks you might receive from your opponent.

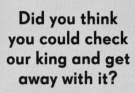

Did you think you could check our king and get away with it?

CAPTURES

After you've looked for checks, ask yourself if you can capture any of your opponent's pieces or if they can capture any of yours. Here you can see that the black pawn on c6 has just captured the white bishop on b5.

THREATS

After you've looked for checks and captures, see if you can threaten to take any of your opponent's other pieces. Here, white moved their bishop from c1 to g5, threatening to take the black queen on their next move. Now that it's black's turn to go, they need to be careful or they will lose their queen! You should also be on the lookout for any threats that may come your way.

I'd better call for backup otherwise I'll be captured!

FOLLOW THE SYSTEM

1. WHAT IS MY OPPONENT DOING?

It's easy to think only about what *your* game plan is, but that won't get you very far. You need to figure out what your opponent is trying to do too! That way you can defend yourself from attacks and prevent your opponent from making moves that could give them an advantage in the game.

2. LOOK FOR CHECKS, CAPTURES, AND THREATS

Once you've figured out what your opponent is trying to do, focus on looking for checks, captures, and threats. Do this before every move you make. Your ability to do so can make or break a game. Flip back to pages 50–51 if you need to refresh your memory.

You've now learned about checks, captures, and threats—but these aren't the only things that can happen during a chess game. You have to be prepared for everything! To make things easier there is a system you can follow to make sure all bases are covered. Following the steps below will help you to make better decisions and improve as a player. Let's dive in!

3. IMPROVE YOUR POSITION

If you can't see any checks, captures, or threats, what should you do? Great question! You can improve the position of your pieces. This simply means moving one of your pieces to a better square than the one it was on before.

It is white's turn to make a move. They can't spot any checks, captures, or threats. What should they do next?

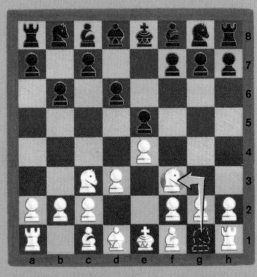

They can improve the knight's position by moving it from g1 to f3. The knight is now in the center of the board and ready for action.

CHAMPIONSHIPS

Who doesn't love some healthy competition? Chess championships take place all over the world—you can probably find one near you! They vary in size and difficulty, from local junior competitions to the World Chess Championship. Maybe you'll compete at one some day...

GRANDMASTERS

Grandmasters are like the gods of chess—these people have worked their socks off to achieve this title. To be a Grandmaster you must have a phenomenally high chess rating. You get this by beating high-profile players in major tournaments. There are around 2,000 Grandmasters.

THE BEST OF THE BEST

The World Chess Championship takes place every two years, and it is the biggest event in the world of chess. The first tournament took place in 1886, when Wilhelm Steinitz came out victorious. Very few players have ever claimed this prestigious title.

MAGNUS CARLSEN

Magnus is considered one of the greatest chess players of all time. He became World Chess Champion in 2013 by defeating the Indian Grandmaster Viswanathan Anand. Find out more about Magnus on pages 104–105.

THE OPENING

Every good story has a beginning, a middle, and an ending. The same is true in chess! The first few moves of every chess game are known as the opening. At this stage it's a good idea to move your pieces closer to the center of the board, so they can more easily attack your opponent. To do this, your pawns need to move forward so your other pieces can then make their moves. It's also a good idea to castle your king (see pages 44–45) in the opening.

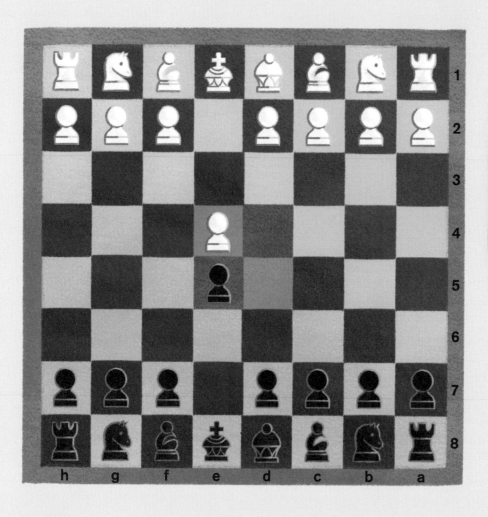

Remember that pawns can advance two squares on their first move. Doing that will allow you to control the center of the board more easily.

PAWN POWER!

These little fellas are fearless! Move them forward as soon as you can. Not only do they start the battle, but moving them opens up space for your other pieces to join in, too. For this reason, it's a good idea to move your pawns on d7 and e7 (if you're playing as black) and d2 and e2 (if you're playing as white), because this enables your bishops to join the party. However, do so carefully—protect your pawns when you can.

KNIGHTS ARE UP

Knights don't mind if the pawns haven't moved out of the way—they can jump over them! In the opening, try to move your knights toward the center of the board—so they have lots of options for their next move. For black, this means ideally moving them to c6 and f6. For white, the goal is to move them to c3 and f3. Remember that a knight is like an octopus with eight arms—if it's in a good spot, it can reach eight different squares (see pages 10–11).

PREPARE YOUR BISHOPS

Bishops can move across the board faster than knights, so it's a good strategy to get them moving early on. Remember that bishops need open diagonal paths to move, so be careful not to block the bishops with your pawns! In this example, your bishop on f8 is free to roam on the diagonal to its right, but the pawn on g7 is blocking the diagonal to its left.

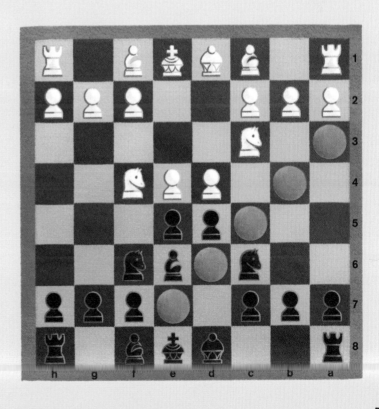

THE MIDDLEGAME

If you're reading this, it means you made it through the opening of the game. Once you've moved a few pawns and got some of your more important pieces off the back rank and into the game, you've entered the middlegame. This is—drumroll please—the middle of the game. Your goal now is to attack your opponent.

CREATE A GAME PLAN

1 Repeat after me: I will look for checks, captures, and threats. Say it again! It's important to look for CCTs every time you make a move. That's the best way to guarantee that you're not missing anything important.

2 What should you do if you can't find any CCTs? Can you remember the system we talked about on pages 52–53? You can still improve your position by moving a piece to a better spot. Repeat these two steps all the way through the middlegame.

TEST IT OUT

Now that you know what to do in the middlegame, let's put that knowledge to the test! Look at this typical example of a middlegame—both players have moved their pieces forward and captured a few of their opponent's pieces. What move should black play next?

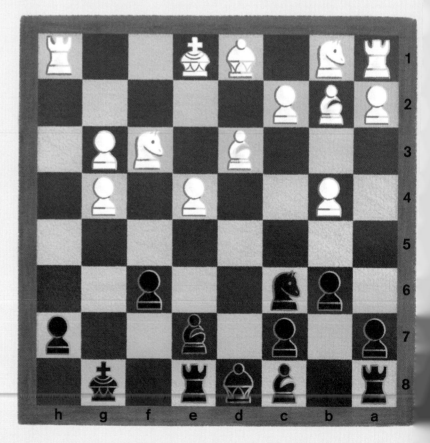

GOOD OPTION

If you said black should move their knight on c6 to b4, you're getting the hang of it! This is a good option because it means they can capture a pawn. However, there is a better move they could have played. Can you spot it?

Told you moving me toward the center would pay off!

GREAT OPTION

If you said they should have moved their bishop from e7 to b4, well done! This is a better move. It allows them to capture a pawn, but more importantly, it puts the white king in check!

That's not bad for a knight, but look how far I can go.

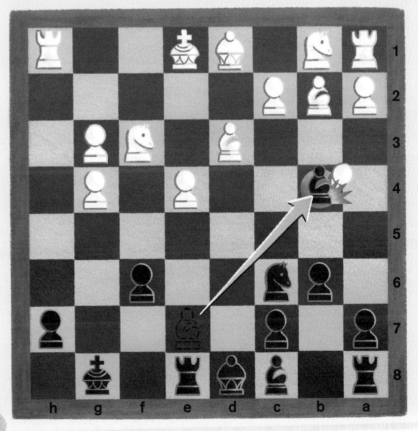

THE ENDGAME

You're now at the end of the game! Well, not exactly. Remember—the game only ends with checkmate. The endgame refers to the latter stages of the game, when most of the pieces have been captured and are no longer on the board. The aim of the endgame is to checkmate your opponent's king, and there are some tricks you can use to help you achieve this!

It's my time to shine!

RUN, KING, RUN!

An endgame with two kings and a pawn is not uncommon. In this example, it is white to move. The black pawn at b2 has a chance to be promoted to a queen if it can reach the end of the board, so the white king must try to take it out before then.

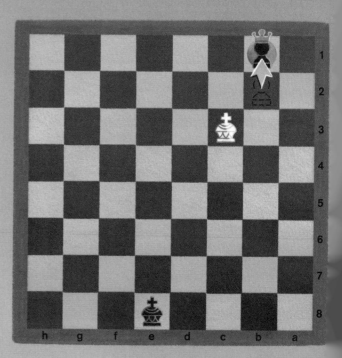

TOO LITTLE, TOO LATE

Promoting that pawn is black's best shot at winning. Will the white king reach the black pawn in time to stop it? Nope! The black pawn reaches b1 and is promoted to a queen.

POWER AT LAST

The endgame is when the king becomes a more powerful and active piece. As there are fewer pieces on the board, the king can roam around more freely without worrying as much about being checkmated. Remember he can also capture any piece, so that white rook on b6 had better watch out!

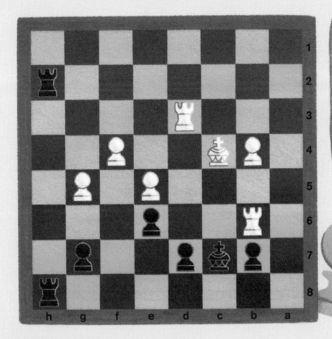

Think back to the king game on pages 42–43. I bet some of the skills you picked up there will help you in the endgame.

HERE COMES THE QUEEN

The white king was too slow and now he has to deal with a black queen. He'd better make a run for it!

With a queen now on the board, black should win easily.

THE BEST PLAYERS

It's time to check in with some more legendary chess players. Get ready to meet a champion who showed men that women were more than a match for men, the genius player she inspired, and a chess player who was as fond of kitties as he was checkmates. The achievements of the players on these pages are an inspiration to us all!

VERA MENCHIK

Born in Moscow, Russia, Vera (1906–1944) was a chess superstar. In 1927 she became the very first Women's World Champion! Her incredible talent was undeniable, and, unusually for the time, she was regularly invited to men's events. She occasionally made quick work of famous male players of the day, including World Champion Max Euwe.

ALEXANDER ALEKHINE

Do you love cats? You're not alone. Alexander (1892–1946), the fourth World Champion, was so fond of cats that he would bring them to tournaments with him! One of his cats was even called Chess! You might think it would be distracting, but Alexander was a dynamite chess player. He was a very aggressive opponent who even had a chess opening named after him!

CHESS

ELIZAVETA BYKOVA

Elizaveta (1913–1989) began playing chess in what is now Russia at the age of 12. She became a Grandmaster, winning the Moscow Women's Chess Championship, the Soviet Women's Chess Championship, and then the biggie—the Women's World Championship—not just once but twice! In her spare time she wrote books—including one about Vera.

Solve the

PUZZLE

Have you been paying attention? It's time for another chess puzzle! For this one it's important to think a couple of moves ahead.

 You're playing with the white pieces.

 Your opponent is playing with the black pieces.

Mine!

Whose turn is it?

STATUS OF THE GAME

It's your turn to make a move, so first scan the board for checks, captures, and threats. When looking for checks, consider all of your options, even if they seem crazy at first. Can you see how you could checkmate your opponent in two moves?

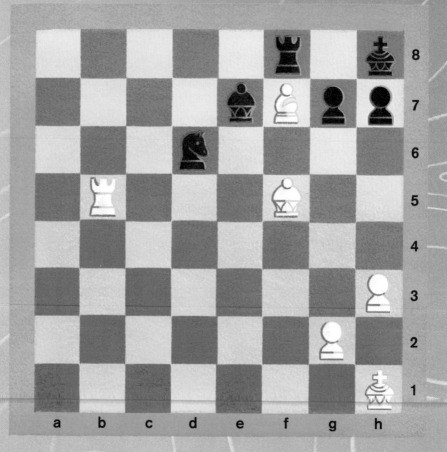

You should check the king by moving your queen on f5 to h7. This looks like a queen sacrifice to me. Will it be worth it?

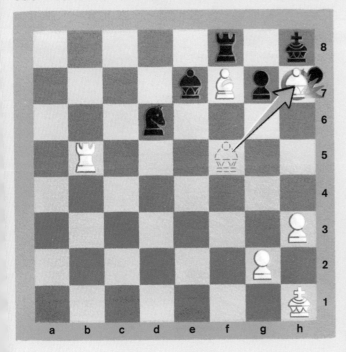

The black king on h8 captures your queen on h7. You lost your queen but you can now win the game with one move. Which piece are you going to move?

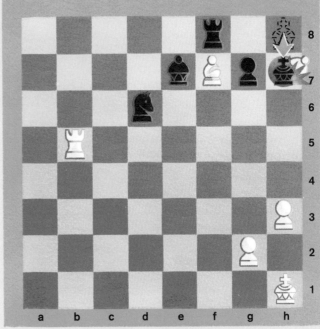

Did you find the move? By moving your rook on b5 to h5 it's checkmate! Black can't capture your rook or protect their king. Your bishop on f7 means their king can't run away to g6 or g8 either. Well done!

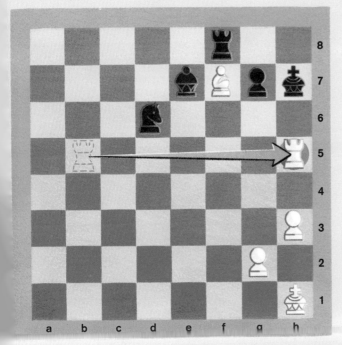

Nowhere to run, Your Majesty!

FIND YOUR STYLE

How you play chess is up to you. Different players have different styles that suit their personalities. Chess styles are a bit like ice cream flavors—everyone has a favorite and there is no right answer! Your style will help you determine how you start and play your games. Which one sounds like you?

TACTICAL AND AGGRESSIVE

If you love going for quick checkmates, this could be the style for you. You like setting traps for your opponents and you can't resist an all-out attack. After all, those are super fun! This style is my personal favorite.

SOLID AND POSITIONAL

This style is all about control. You're not aggressive when attacking and quick checkmates aren't a priority for you. You like to carefully and slowly plot a path to victory, then strike when the time is right, taking no risks. You don't shy away from long games.

GETTING A HEAD START

It can be hard to know the best way to start a chess game because most of your pieces are stuck behind pawns. Luckily, you can play tried and tested sequences of moves that allow you to make a clever start—we call these "openings" (not to be confused with the opening of the game—see pages 56–57). Let's run through an opening called the London System—named after a famous tournament in London where lots of players used it.

1. THE PAWN STEPS UP

You're playing as white, so you have the first move. It's best to start by moving one of your central pawns—the ones on d2 and e2—to the center of the board. Here, you've moved the pawn on d2 to d4.

2. PAWN FACE-OFF

If black responded by moving a pawn from e7 to e5 or from c7 to c5, you could easily capture that pawn. Instead, black moves a pawn from d7 to d5.

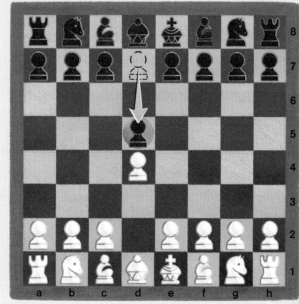

3. THE KNIGHT'S TURN

The next step is to use a piece that can jump over pawns—the knight! Move the knight on g1 to f3.

4. TOUCHÉ

Now you've moved one of your pieces off the back rank, your opponent will probably do the same. Black moves their knight from g8 to f6.

5. CALLING THE BISHOP

The next move in the London System is to bring a bishop into play. Because there isn't a pawn on d2 you can move the bishop on c1 to f4—it's ready to battle!

WHAT HAPPENS NEXT?

Well, that's anyone's guess! At this point the opening has served its purpose—you've moved powerful pieces into good positions early in the game, and there's not much black can do to stop it.

FAMOUS OPENINGS

Aggressive openings

There are hundreds of chess openings. Some are more suited to players with an aggressive style, while others are favorites among players with a positional style (who like to be more cautious). Try out a few to see which ones you like best!

THE ITALIAN GAME

This opening allows white to get their g1 knight and f1 bishop off the back rank quickly. This means they can castle their king early on.

THE MODERN DEFENSE

White starts every game, but that doesn't mean black can't have openings, too! After white does their thing, black moves a pawn from g7 to g6 so they can move their f8 bishop to g7 with their next move. This opening keeps white guessing as to what black will do next.

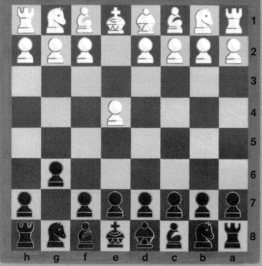

THE SCOTCH GAME

The Scotch Game is for aggressive players. White uses the central pawns and the g1 knight to dominate the center of the board.

THE QUEEN'S GAMBIT

This is one of the most popular openings in chess. White moves the d2 pawn to d4. If black moves their pawn to d5, white moves the c2 pawn to c4. If the black pawn takes the pawn on c4, it moves the black pawn out of the center of the board, giving white an advantage despite sacrificing a piece.

You know what to do, right?

Of course, Your Majesty.

Over my dead body!

THE QUEEN'S GAMBIT DECLINED

If you're playing as black and your opponent opens with the Queen's Gambit, you can defend yourself with this opening. After they advance their pawns, move your pawn from e7 to e6. This will defend your pawn on d5 and stop the attack.

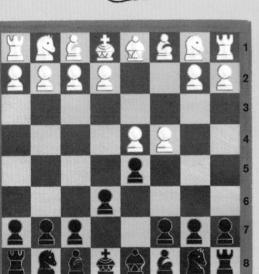

THE FRENCH DEFENSE

The French Defense is a strong defensive opening for black. After white moves a pawn to e4, black responds by first moving the e7 pawn one square to e6, then another pawn to d5. These pawns now have each other's backs!

THE CHECKMATE TRAP

Chess can be a hard game to win, so it doesn't hurt to have a few tricks up your sleeve! You can gain an advantage in a match by setting traps for your opponent. Like every good trap, the ones you're about to learn require careful planning.

You're playing as white, so you're up first. Start by moving your pawn from e2 to e4 so you can control some squares in the center. Your opponent will probably do the same thing.

Next, push your bishop at f1 to c4 so it can threaten the black pawn on f7. From here, your opponent can make a number of moves, such as moving their knight from b8 to c6.

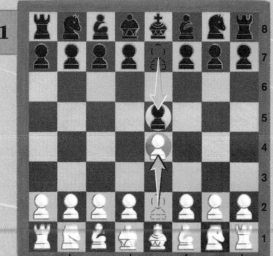

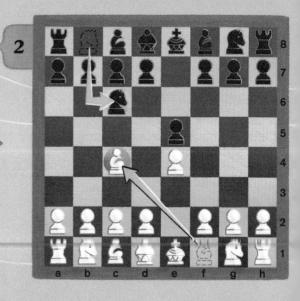

Listen up, class! Your first lesson is on how to set a trap for a quick checkmate known as Scholar's Mate. Remember: your pieces need to work as a team.

Move your queen to h5 so it can also threaten the black pawn on f7. That's what we call teamwork! Hopefully your opponent moves their other knight to f6 so it can attack your queen, falling into your trap...

Your queen now takes the pawn on f7 and checkmates. I told you that would be quick!

THE BISHOP AND KNIGHT TRAP

You don't just have to use tricks and traps to checkmate your opponent, you can also use them to capture other valuable pieces. This trap involves your bishop and your knight.

You're playing with the white pieces. Start by playing your pawn on e2 to e4, taking control of the center of the board. Your opponent moves their pawn at e7 to e5.

1

Move your knight on f3 up to g5, which threatens the f7 pawn again! That f7 pawn is already being attacked by your bishop on c4. At this stage it is very common for your opponent to not spot this and instead attack your knight at g5 by moving their pawn from h7 to h6. They have no idea what's coming their way!

With your knight at g5, take the pawn on f7. Now your knight is in position to attack two different pieces—the queen on d8 and the rook on h8. If your opponent moves the queen, you take the rook. If they move the rook, you take the queen.

4

5

Next, move your knight on g1 to f3.
Your opponent's pawn is now in danger,
so they will probably do something about
it! They move their knight on b8 to c6,
which defends the pawn on e5.

On your turn,
move your bishop on
f1 to c4, eyeing up your
opponent's pawn on f7.
They play their knight on
g8 to f6, which puts
your e4 pawn in
danger.

Your opponent
decides to move their
queen to e7, where it is
safe. You can then capture
the rook on h8, winning a
very powerful piece!

THE COPYCAT TRAP

If you're playing as white, you're always the one to make the first move. That means every once in a while you'll be up against someone who just copies your every move! Their lack of creativity can be annoying, but you can use it to your advantage.

Move your pawn at e2 to e4. You're dealing with a copycat, so your opponent matches your move with a pawn to e5.

Move your queen to e2, so it's in position to attack the knight on e4. You want your opponent to move their knight out of harm's way.

That's exactly what they do—they retreat their knight to f6. Now move your knight to c6 so it can attack the black queen. But that's not all! Take a look at the white queen on e2—it's now checking the black king! Your opponent is forced to respond to the check.

Next, move your knight at g1 to f3 so it's in position to attack the pawn at e5. You guessed it—your opponent does the same and moves their knight at g8 to f6, attacking your pawn on e4.

Take their pawn on e5 with your knight. They will do the same, capturing your pawn on e4 with their knight. Don't worry though: this is when you set the trap!

One way your opponent can block the check is by moving their queen to e7. If that's the move they make, you can take their queen with your knight.

Alternatively, they could move their bishop on f8 to e7 so it blocks the check. If that's what they do, take their queen on d8 with your knight. Whatever happens, that copycat has lost their queen!

OR

THE QUEEN TRAP

A good rule of thumb in chess is not to move your queen too early in the game, but there are exceptions to this. In this sneaky trap, I'll teach you how to use your queen early on to attack multiple pieces at once—while keeping her safe, of course!

Make a bold move and bring out your queen to h5. This will probably surprise your opponent. Your queen can now attack the black pawn on e5. How do you think your opponent will react?

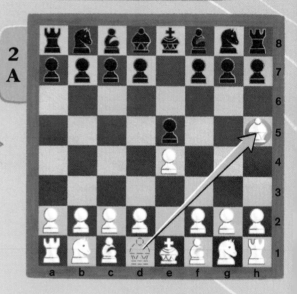

OR

Here is the second option. You move your queen to h5, but instead of moving their knight your opponent moves their pawn on g7 to g6. The pawn is threatening your queen and it's backed up by other pawns. If you capture the pawn you'll lose your queen. What can you do instead?

Start by moving your white pawn on e2 to e4. Your opponent moves their pawn at e7 to e5. There are two ways you can set the queen trap.

78

Your opponent moves their knight on g8 to f6 so it can attack your queen. Was this the best move?

Nope! You can take their pawn on e5 with your queen, without losing any pieces. More importantly, your opponent is now in check!

3 A

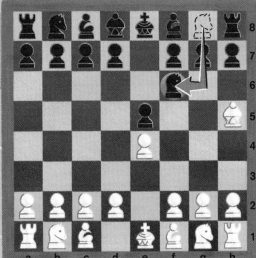

4 A

Take the pawn on e5 with your queen. Not only is this check, but their rook in the corner on h8 is now under threat as well. It's a double attack! Your opponent moves their bishop on f8 to e7 to protect the king, but that doesn't help their rook...

You can now take their rook on h8! If your opponent falls for this trap, you'll have a big advantage and a good chance to win the game.

3 B

4 B

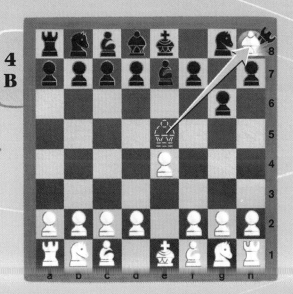

Solve the

PUZZLE

Are you ready for another chess puzzle? Make sure you look at the whole board for the best possible move and don't rush into any decisions.

 You're playing with the black pieces.

 Your opponent is playing with the white pieces.

Whose turn is it?

Mine!

STATUS OF THE GAME

There's a tempting move on the board, can you spot it? If you move your bishop at c5 to f2, you can put white's king in check. However, this wouldn't be a great move. The king would be able to capture your bishop and get away with it unharmed—you don't want that! Just because you can check, doesn't mean you always have to. What move should you make instead?

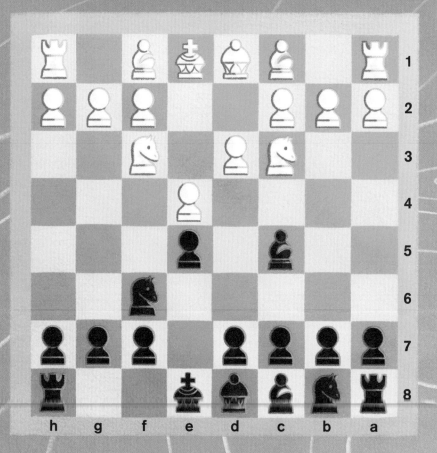

The best option is moving the knight on f6 to g4.
Did you spot it? Now the white pawn on f2 is under
threat from the knight on g4 and the bishop on c5.

Don't worry about that black knight. We're totally safe back here!

White moves their pawn on h2 to h3,
threatening your knight on g4. If you
don't respond, they could capture it.
Where should your knight go?

You should take the pawn
on f2 with your knight on g4.
The white king can't capture
your knight because your
bishop on c5 is defending
it. Good job!

Remember that pieces work best when they work together. Here we've set a trap for white using our knight and bishop. If white moves the rook on h1, we take the queen. If white moves the queen on d1, we take the rook.

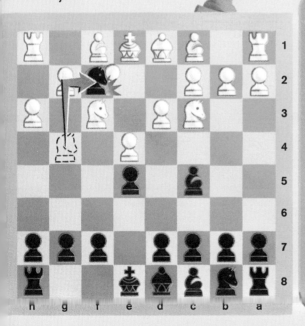

THE FORBIDDEN GAME

Chess and religion haven't always seen eye to eye. At different points in history, chess has been banned by religions including Christianity, Islam, and Judaism. Some religious leaders thought the game involved violence or encouraged gambling. Not everyone agreed with this. In fact, the first modern chess book was written by a Catholic priest called Rodrigo "Ruy" López de Segura. He even has a chess opening named after him!

THE FOLDING CHESSBOARD

Just because chess bans were in place, it didn't mean they always worked... One priest wanted to play so badly, he invented a folding board that could be hidden in plain sight! It looked like two books stacked together. To this day we don't know his name, but we have a lot to thank him for.

THE BEST PLAYERS

For our next roundup of chess superstars we'll meet a player with a voice as good as his chess openings, a swimming speedster, and a player who had to overcome incredible adversity to make it to the top.

MIKHAIL TAL

If you thought your chess tricks were good, you should check out Mikhail Tal (1936–1992), also known as the Magician from Riga! This guy was known for his traps and sacrifices. He was super aggressive and is one of my all-time favorites! Mikhail was the eighth World Champion.

VASILY SMYSLOV

Vasily (1921–2010) was the seventh World Champion. He was nicknamed The Hand, because it was said that when he moved a piece, he knew exactly where he should place it, with barely any calculation. When he wasn't playing chess, Vasily liked to sing opera!

LYUDMILA RUDENKO

Say hello to the second Women's World Champion! Lyudmila (1904–1986) came from a part of the Soviet Union that is now in Ukraine. Fun fact: Lyudmila was a competitive swimmer before she was a player. Her playing style was very, *very* aggressive. Maybe something she learned from swimming competitions?

CHESS CHAMPIONSHIPS

TIGRAN PETROSIAN

Now we have a real rags-to-riches story. As a youngster, Tigran Petrosian (1929–1984) had to sweep the streets to make a living, all while developing a love for chess in his spare time. It paid off—in 1963 Tigran became the ninth champion of the world. At one point he went unbeaten in tournaments for a whole year!

DRAWING A GAME

We'd all love to win every single game of chess we play, but sadly that's just not possible! We either win, lose, or draw. In chess there are three main ways in which a game ends in a draw. Let's find out what they are!

STALEMATE

A stalemate happens when it's a player's turn but they can't make any moves. They have nowhere to go because their opponent is blocking all of the squares they could otherwise move to. Stalemates usually happen toward the end of the game, but they can also happen with lots of pieces still on the board.

In this example of a stalemate, it's black to move. Hang on a second... The white queen on g6 is preventing the black king from moving anywhere! If he did, he would be putting himself in check and that's not allowed. He's stuck!

Black also can't move in this example. Take a look—every single black piece is being blocked by other pieces! The black king can't go to c8 because he would be putting himself in check. The result? Stalemate.

50 MOVES

When there are lots of moves back and forth, without either side really getting anywhere, the game can end in a draw because of something called the 50-move rule. This rule says that after 50 moves without any captures or pawns advancing, the game ends in a draw. These games are very long!

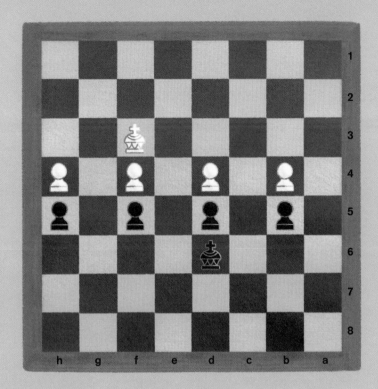

NOT ENOUGH PIECES LEFT

A draw can also happen when neither player can checkmate their opponent's king because there aren't enough pieces on the board to do so. The most common example is a king versus king duel. The game ends in a draw because kings can't checkmate each other.

Solve the
PUZZLE

Are you ready to put on your thinking hat for another chess puzzle? Here's a hint for solving this one: don't be afraid to make sacrifices. If planned carefully, they can be game changers.

You're playing with the black pieces.

Your opponent is playing with the white pieces.

Mine!

Whose turn is it?

STATUS OF THE GAME

You're in the endgame and there aren't many pieces left on the board. Can you see how you can checkmate the white king in two moves?

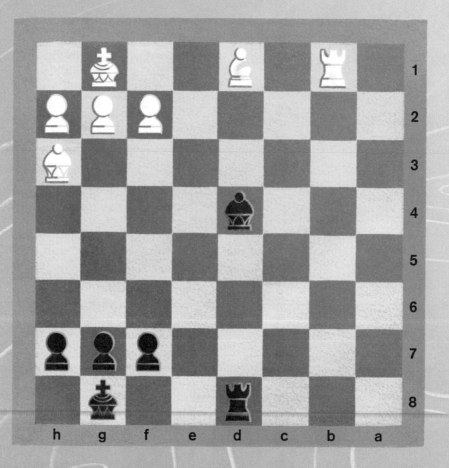

The first step is to move the black queen from d4 to d1 to capture the white bishop and check the king on g1. You're putting your queen in danger, but it'll be worth it.

Always think ahead!

White captures your queen and gets out of check by moving their rook from b1 to d1. What should you do next? Don't let that sacrifice go to waste!

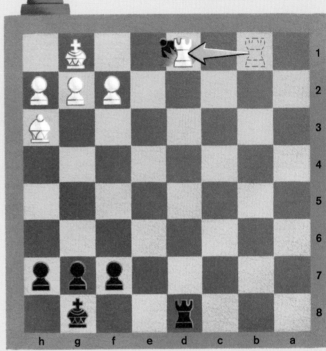

Did you move your rook from d8 to d1 to capture the white rook? If so, well done—that's checkmate. Losing the queen was worth it!

LONG–DISTANCE CHESS

Today, you can play chess with someone on the other side of the world in real time thanks to technology, but that wasn't the case in the past. Those who lived far away from each other had to get creative! The solution? Correspondence chess. People used letters, fax machines, and even homing pigeons to play—some still do! It could take days to know whether or not your opponent fell for your trap...

FAX MACHINES

If two people had fax machines, they could play chess against each other from anywhere in the world. These machines could scan a piece of paper with your move written on it, and your opponent's machine would print it out for them!

PEN PALS

Have you ever written a letter to a friend who lives in a different country? That's how some people used to play chess. The oldest postal chess game was played back in 1804! Sealed inside each envelope would be a chess move—matches could take months!

Some long-distance chess players use **homing pigeons** to send their **moves** to each other!

BAD MOVE, EARTH

In 1970, Russian cosmonauts on board the Soyuz 9 spacecraft challenged players on Earth to a game of chess. Six hours and three orbits around Earth later, the game ended in a draw. In 2020, astronauts aboard the International Space Station played chess to celebrate the anniversary of the Soyuz 9 game.

BOARD VISION

In a game of chess it's important to keep track of all the pieces on the board, all the time! This is called board vision. There are usually multiple things going on at once in a game, so to avoid making mistakes, keep those eyes peeled!

TEAM EFFORT

If you take one thing away from this book let it be this: chess is a team game! You are more likely to win when you use your pieces together. When you're looking for your next move, ask yourself how you can use more than one piece to set a trap or attack your opponent's pieces.

TWO IS BETTER THAN ONE

Using one piece to threaten one of your opponent's pieces is a good start, but using two pieces is even better! It's white's turn to move in this example—which two white pieces are working together? The knight on b5 and the bishop on f4 are both attacking the pawn on c7. If one doesn't capture it, the other will! Black can say goodbye to that pawn.

CHECKMATE

It is possible to checkmate using only one piece, but the majority of checkmates are done with several pieces. In this example, the white queen on f7 is checking the black king on e8. If she was acting alone, the black king would be able to capture her. But that's not the case—she has backup! The white knight on g5 is protecting the queen. This means the black king can't get out of check. Game over!

THE BEST PLAYERS

To become a Grandmaster, you need to be incredibly smart and work really hard. On these pages you'll meet the sisters who conquered the world of women's chess, arguably the best player of all time, and a player who inspired an entire country to take up chess.

GARRY KASPAROV

To many people across the world, Garry Kasparov (born 1963) is considered the greatest player of all time. He became the youngest ever World Champion in 1985, when he was just 22! At one point he was the world's highest-rated player ever, with a rating of 2851. Ratings in chess reflect a player's skill level—the higher the rating, the better the player.

VISWANATHAN ANAND

Viswanathan (born 1969) was the first ever Indian Grandmaster and a true trailblazer. His success inspired a chess boom in India, lighting a burning passion for the game that continues to this day. Viswanathan was the fifteenth World Champion. He was also one of the few players to achieve a rating above 2800, peaking at 2817. What a legend!

MIKHAIL BOTVINNIK

For some people, chess is their whole life, but other chess players have more than one passion. Mikhail (1911–1995) was a Grandmaster from the Soviet Union and the sixth World Champion—a title he held for almost 15 years. On top of that, he was a world-class electrical engineer! Mikhail also founded the legendary Soviet Chess School, which produced three more World Champions: Anatoly Karpov, Vladimir Kramnik, and Garry Kasparov.

THE POLGÁR SISTERS

Meet Judit, Susan, and Sofia. The Polgár sisters were chess prodigies who were intensely trained by their father. It paid off—Judit (born 1976) and Susan (born 1969) became Grandmasters, and Sofia (born 1971) became an International Master (the level below Grandmaster). Judit is considered the best female player of all time, while Susan was a Women's World Champion. This is probably the strongest chess family ever!

WATCH THE CLOCK

Most chess games today are played with a time limit. In a timed game, a chess clock tells you how long you have left to make all your moves. The clock starts counting down at the beginning of the game. If you run out of time, you lose! There are different time limits, which means some matches last for hours, while others are over in two minutes!

FOREVER AND EVER

Imagine you are playing against someone who is clearly about to lose and instead of admitting defeat they just sit there—for hours! Annoying, right? Timed games stop this from happening.

ADDING TIME

If the thought of playing a timed game gives you the chills, never fear! It's possible to have time added back on to your clock using what we call increments. In this type of chess, every time you make a move and hit the clock a few seconds are added back on. Your overall time is still counting down, but it gives you a few more seconds to think and an incentive to play quickly. The most popular increments are five or ten seconds added after every move.

Hit your clock after every move you make. This pauses your time and restarts your opponent's time.

The rules of the game are always the same no matter what time limit you're playing with.

BLINK AND YOU'LL MISS IT

Can you imagine a chess game only lasting two minutes? Welcome to bullet chess. Picture pieces flying around as players desperately try to hit the chess clock—bullet chess is wild!

DON'T PANIC!

Keep an eye on your clock—be aware of how much time you have left and use it wisely. My tip? Stay calm. Timed games can be a lot of pressure, but you need to take some time to think about your next move. Chess is a thinking game after all!

THE COLD WAR

Between 1946 and 1991, the two most powerful nations on Earth clashed for supremacy. It was a tense period, but the USA and the Soviet Union (modern-day Russia and several surrounding countries) didn't ever fight each other on a battlefield. As a result, the conflict was known as the Cold War. In 1972, American Bobby Fischer and Russian Boris Spassky played each other in a chess match that became known as the match of the century. They were fighting for a lot more than the title of World Chess Champion.

THE SOVIET UNION

For more than five decades, the Soviet Union had dominated the world of chess. For them, chess was a symbol of pride and dominance. Boris Spassky knew that a defeat would be a huge disappointment for his country.

POLITICS ON THE LINE

In 1972, Richard Nixon was the president of the USA and Leonid Brezhnev was the leader of the Soviet Union. Both men knew that a win on the chessboard would be a hugely symbolic moment for the victorious country.

THE USA

The match lasted six weeks, and Bobby Fischer came out victorious, claiming the title of World Chess Champion. His triumph was received with great joy in the USA. It started a chess boom that can still be seen today.

SUPER DEFENSE

Some people say that attack is the best form of defense. In chess, that's not always true. Defending your pieces is just as important as attacking your opponent's pieces. If you only focus on building a plan of attack, you risk losing valuable pieces—or worse, being checkmated. I'm going to teach you two ways you can defend yourself against an enemy attack.

MAKE A RUN FOR IT

One of the ways to avoid being captured is to move out of harm's way. On the board below, the white pawn on e5 is threatening to take your knight on f6. What should you do? You could move the knight back to its starting position on g8, but that would mean undoing the progress you've made. The best option is to move it to d7, where it's safe but still ready for action.

Think carefully about which pieces are worth defending. Losing a pawn isn't as bad as losing a rook!

CALL FOR BACKUP

Sometimes you can make your opponent think twice before capturing one of your vulnerable pieces, by protecting it with another piece. Look at the example below—white is attacking your pawn on e5 with their knight on f3. Your pawn is blocked by the white pawn on e4 and can't go anywhere, so your best form of defense is to use another pawn to try and stop your opponent from taking it. You can move your pawn on d7 to d6. Now if the white knight tries to take the pawn on e5, you'll take it down with your backup pawn!

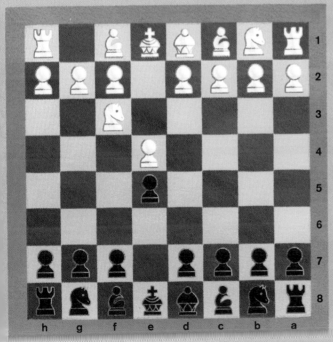

THE BEST PLAYERS

It's the last of our roundups of the best players of all time. Hopefully you've found some heroes in these pages that can inspire you. But these are just a few champions! There are plenty more out there. Find someone you like and study their games—you'll be amazed how much it can help!

ANATOLY KARPOV

Anatoly (born 1951) was the twelfth World Champion and was nicknamed the Boa Constrictor because of his playing style. He was careful with the positioning of his pieces, slowly squeezing his opponent with clever moves until they succumbed, just like a real boa constrictor!

NONA GAPRINDASHVILI

Nona (born 1941) is a legendary women's chess player. In 1978 she became the first female Grandmaster. She was the fifth Women's World Champion and successfully defended her title four times. She grew up in what is now Georgia, a country in Eastern Europe where football was really popular. Her achievements were so great that the local team—Dinamo Tbilisi—even came to see her play!

MAGNUS CARLSEN

Along with Garry Kasparov, Magnus (born 1990) is considered one of the greatest of the greats. A former prodigy from Norway, he became one of the youngest Grandmasters ever at 13 years old! For years Magnus dominated the world of chess. But every champion's time must eventually end... Who will take his place at the top?

JU WENJUN

Ju Wenjun (born 1991) is a Chinese Grandmaster. She started playing chess when she was seven years old and in 2018 claimed the title of Women's World Champion. When she was young, Wenjun lived in a training center full of brilliant chess players just like her. Can you imagine being neighbors with a world champion?

CHESS TRAINING CENTER

Solve the
PUZZLE

You know the drill by now! First, look at the whole board. Then look more closely to see if you can check, capture any pieces, or threaten your opponent. Circle back to pages 50–51 if you need a refresher.

 You're playing with the white pieces.

 Your opponent is playing with the black pieces.

Mine!

Whose turn is it?

STATUS OF THE GAME

It's still early in the game. Black has just used their queen to take your knight that was on d4. Was bringing their queen out early a mistake? Is there anything you can do to take advantage of that? What's your next move?

The best move here is to move your bishop on d3 to b5, checking the black king! Look at the two queens now—they're staring at each other. Someone is about to lose their queen... Lucky for you, it's black's turn to move and their king is in check.

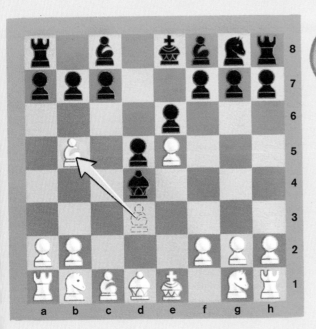

Not so fast! Your king is in check so you need to deal with that first.

Black decides to block the check by moving their bishop from c8 to d7.

Now you can take their queen with your queen. Or, better still, check their king by capturing their bishop on d7 (and sacrificing your bishop to their king), before coming back for the queen. Either way, the black queen is yours!

PARK PLAYTIME

Today we can play chess virtually anywhere thanks to our phones, tablets, and computers. But if you ask me, one of the most fun places to play chess is in parks. These outdoor spaces are safe havens for people to chat, play, claim victory, admit defeat, and have fun—a chess party in the park! There are famous chess parks dotted around some of the biggest cities in the world. Why don't you see if there are any chess parks in your neighborhood?

MIX AND MATCH

Playing chess outdoors brings communities together—anyone can challenge anyone! You will probably play against people of different ages and from different backgrounds. Over time, this is a great way to build new friendships. You can even find chess clubs in some parks.

GIANT CHESS, ANYONE?

Did you know that some chess pieces are so big they come up to your shoulders? Welcome to the world of giant chess! This game is played on huge boards and players have to pick up the pieces with both hands to move them. If you are playing a timed game you can end up running across the board— it's quite the workout!

COMPUTER CHESS

- -

Computers have enhanced so many areas of our lives,
and chess is no exception! Technology has helped everyone
improve their chess skills—from Grandmasters to beginners.
When the first chess computer programs were made, humans
could beat the computers. Now we don't stand
a chance against them!

THE FIRST PROGRAM

The British computer scientist (and war hero) Alan Turing
reckoned he could teach a computer to play chess, and
boy was he right! In 1948 he developed a simple chess
program called Turochamp. In theory it could plan two to
four chess moves ahead. However, the computers of the
time weren't powerful enough to run the program properly,
so Alan used the computer code he had written to play
chess himself. Nevertheless, he had made a crucial first
move in the development of computer chess.

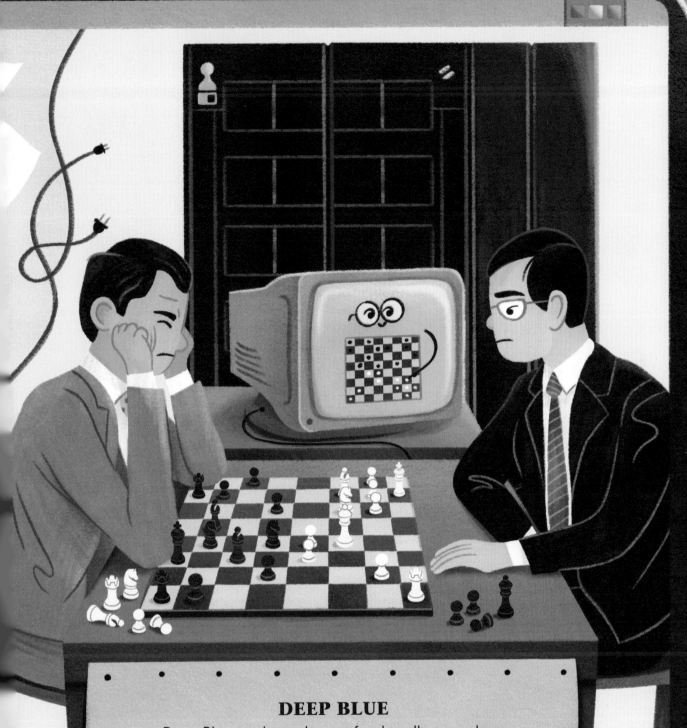

DEEP BLUE

Deep Blue is a legendary artificial intelligence chess program. It was developed by a company called IBM and represented a breakthrough in computer chess. In a famous match in 1996, it was pitted against the Grandmaster Garry Kasparov. It lost, but the next year it was upgraded and took him on again. In this battle of man versus machine, Deep Blue won! It was a huge moment and showed the enormous possibilities of artificial intelligence.

MEET THE PRODIGIES

PAUL MORPHY

This child prodigy was considered the first great American chess player. He was born in 1837 and learned how to play chess by just watching! By the time he was 20, he was considered one of the best chess players in the world.

JOSÉ RAÚL CAPABLANCA

José was taught to play chess in Cuba by his father when he was just four. By the age of eight he was playing chess at the Havana Chess Club. At 13 he defeated the Cuban champion, Juan Corzo!

JUDIT POLGÁR

Judit (see also page 97) was a star at a young age and won her first international chess tournament when she was just nine! She was the top-ranked female player in the world at the age of 12—a distinction she held for 26 years until she retired!

A chess prodigy is a kid who has an exceptional ability to play the game at a very young age. Kind of like an adult in a child's body! These kids have been known to beat Grandmasters. Do you think you could be the next chess prodigy?

MAGNUS CARLSEN

Magnus (see also pages 55 and 105) learned how to play chess in Norway when he was five years old. He became an International Master at 12 years old and the second-youngest Grandmaster in history when he was 13.

SAMUEL RESHEVSKY

Samuel learned how to play chess in Poland when he was four. At the age of eight he gave his first simultaneous exhibition, playing several people at the same time! He would later win the US Chess Championships seven times.

BOBBY FISCHER

Bobby (see also pages 100–101) started playing in chess clubs when he was six. At 14 he became the youngest US champion and at 15 he became the then-youngest Grandmaster in history! He went on to become the only American World Chess Champion.

Solve the
PUZZLE

I have one last puzzle for you, chess expert. This one is tricky.
Are you up to the challenge? Use all the lessons you've learned
in this book, and take your time—you've got this!

 You're playing
with the black
pieces.

 Your opponent is
playing with the
white pieces.

Mine!

Whose
turn is it?

STATUS OF THE GAME

There are a lot of pieces on the board, but don't let it
fool you—you can checkmate the white king in two
moves if you're clever. What move should you make?

If you said moving your queen from c7 over to a7, well done! You're setting a trap that will hopefully cost white the game.

White doesn't see the threat coming their way. They move their knight from e2 to f4. This isn't a very smart move. Which move should you make to take advantage of their mistake?

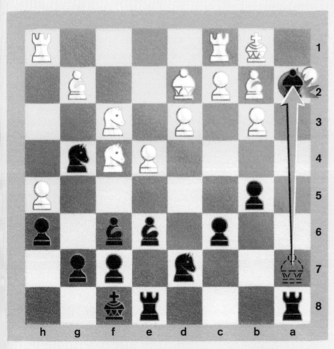

Move your queen from a7 to a2 and take their pawn. This is also checkmate! The white king can't capture your queen because it's protected by your rook on a8. Good game!

CHESS STRATEGIES

1
ALWAYS HAVE A PLAN

A bad plan is better than no plan at all. Think of ways that your pieces can work as a team. A plan can be anything, from moving your pieces to the center of the board to setting traps, or even just stopping one of your opponent's attacks!

2
IMPROVE THE POSITION OF YOUR PIECES

Do you still have valuable pieces on your back row? Move them out! They're not much help to you if you can't use them to start attacks and capture pieces.

3
PROTECT YOUR KING

If your king is checkmated, you lose. If your opponent's king is checkmated, they lose. No wonder he is the most important piece on the board. Protect him in any way you can!

You're almost at the end of the book! Your brain must be overflowing with all of the tips and lessons you've learned. It can feel a bit overwhelming, but don't worry—with time and practice it will all make sense. Until then, here is a recap of some of the most important things you should be thinking about when playing chess.

4 ATTACK, ATTACK, ATTACK

Move your pieces forward to attack your opponent's pieces. Capture their pieces if you can—it'll make checkmating them easier. Go back to pages 56–61 to remember how best to use your pieces in the opening, the middlegame, and the endgame.

5 DO THE MATH

Chess is a team game, but some pieces are more valuable than others. Whenever you are trading pieces, think carefully about whether or not it's a smart move. Make sure you know what fair and unfair trades are. Go back to pages 30–31 if you need a reminder.

6 KEEP YOUR EYES WIDE OPEN

Look at the whole board, all of the time. Remember what you learned about board vision on pages 92–93. If you don't know what's going on everywhere on the board, you won't be able to plan good attacks or defend yourself against your enemy. Good board vision will help you to make fewer mistakes.

QUESTIONS TO REMEMBER

We ask ourselves questions every day: What will I have for dinner? Should I play in the park after school? Why can't I have a later bedtime? It's important to constantly ask yourself questions when you're in the middle of a chess game, too! Here is a checklist of important questions that you should remember to ask when playing.

WHAT IS MY OPPONENT DOING?

Ask yourself this question every time your opponent makes a move. If you can figure out what their plan is, you can try to stop it!

ARE THERE ANY CHECKS, CAPTURES, OR THREATS?

Keep your eyes open for any of these three things before every move— for both you and your opponent.

WHAT IS MY PLAN?

You won't get very far if you don't have a plan. You might get lucky sometimes, but it's a good rule of thumb to have a clear strategy for how you will win.

CAN I CHECKMATE?

Remember that this is how you win the game, so if you can checkmate always go for it!

IS MY OPPONENT ATTACKING ME?

Don't let your guard down! It's wise to know when you're being attacked so you can defend your pieces.

CAN THEY TAKE MY PIECE?

Sacrificing a piece can be worth it if you have a plan. However, avoid giving up your pieces for free. Think about fair trades (pages 30–31).

HOW CAN I IMPROVE MY POSITION?

If you're ever stuck during a game, don't panic! Try moving one of your pieces to a better square than where it was before.

IS MY OPPONENT THREATENING TO CHECKMATE ME?

Always be on high alert! If you think you're about to be checkmated, try to prevent it before it's too late.

IS MY KING SAFE?

No matter what is going on across the board, you should always keep an eye on your king. Make sure he is protected.

PUSHING THE LIMIT

Chess is one of the most popular games in the world. Over the years, extraordinary people have pushed the boundaries of what is possible in this amazing game. Some of them have even set world records!

LONGEST UNDEFEATED STREAK

Between July 31, 2018, and October 9, 2020, Magnus Carlsen played 125 matches. And guess what—he didn't lose a single one! What's the longest you've gone without being checkmated?

GET A MOVE ON!

Ivan Nikolic and Goran Arsovic played a game in 1989 that lasted 269 moves and 20 hours! Someone should have introduced them to bullet chess...

Can you imagine playing chess blindfolded? You have to keep a picture of the whole game in your mind. Some pros can even play multiple games at once while blindfolded!

BLINDFOLD CHESS

LONGEST-REIGNING WORLD CHESS CHAMPION

Emanuel Lasker holds the record for being World Chess Champion for the longest. He was the best player in the world for 27 years!

2882!

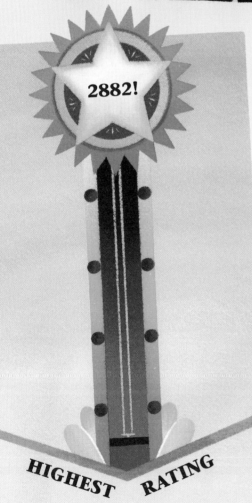

AGE IS JUST A NUMBER

Abhimanyu Mishra is the youngest Grandmaster in history, achieving the title when he was just 12! The oldest Grandmaster was Yuri Averbakh, who was 100 years old.

HIGHEST RATING

The highest chess rating of all time? Look no further than that man again—our friend Magnus Carlsen. In 2014 he achieved a rating of 2882. Reckon you could beat that number one day?

EXTREME CHESS

You play chess at home, at school, in the park—maybe even while sitting on the toilet. For some people this isn't exciting enough, so they play chess while skydiving!

WHAT'S NEXT?

You made it to the end of the book! Of course you did, chess superstar.

The question now is: What should you do next? The best advice I can give you is to flick back to the beginning of the book! Read it over and over again. I guarantee you will spot something new every time. Revisit this book tomorrow, and the day after, and the day after that. The best and quickest way to get better at chess is to keep practicing. The more you play, the more you will improve.

If you have access to a phone or computer, you can play chess against other people online—but you must always be supervised by an adult. If you have a chessboard at home or at school, challenge some friends and family members. Put the skills you just learned to the test. If you lose sometimes, that's okay too. Just keep playing!

I wish you nothing but great chess games, learning, wins, and fun! See ya around!

GLOSSARY

50-MOVE RULE

A rule that states that a game ends in a draw if no pawns have advanced and no pieces have been captured in the last 50 moves.

BISHOP

One of the pieces in a chess game. It can move diagonally forward and backward as short or far as it wants. Each player has two bishops.

BLINDFOLD CHESS

A way of playing chess where one or both players are blindfolded while playing. They have to remember the positions of all of the pieces.

BOARD VISION

The practice of looking at what's going on everywhere on a chessboard during a game.

BULLET CHESS

A format of chess where each player has a minute to make all of their moves.

CASTLING

A special move used to protect a player's king. In one move, players can move their king sideways two spaces and move their rook to the other side of the king.

CHATURANGA

A board game that originated in India nearly 1,500 years ago. Chess evolved from chaturanga.

CHECK

A situation where a player finds their king at risk of being checkmated in the next move by their opponent.

CHECKMATE

A situation where a player's king cannot escape the opponent's pieces. Checkmate is the end of the game.

CORRESPONDENCE CHESS

A long-distance game of chess where moves are communicated by email, fax machines, the mail, or even homing pigeons!

ENDGAME

The last phase of a chess game. In the endgame, there are usually fewer pieces on the board.

FIDE

The International Chess Federation, known by its French name: *Fédération Internationale des Échecs*. An institution that organizes important chess events, including the World Chess Championship.

FILE

A column (vertical line) on a chessboard.

GIANT CHESS

A chess game where all the pieces are extraordinarily big—some could be as tall as you!

GRANDMASTER

The highest possible ranking in chess, given to the best players in the world.

HNEFATAFL

A variation of chess that was played by the Vikings.

KING

The most important piece in a chess game. The king can only move one square at a time. If a king is checkmated, the game is over.

KINGSIDE

Refers to the side of the board the king is on. It is the right side of the board if you're playing as white and the left side of the board if you're playing as black.

KNIGHT

One of the pieces in a chess game. It moves in an L shape. Each player has two knights.

LONG-RANGE PIECE

A chess piece that can move several squares across the board in one move. Bishops, rooks, and queens are long-range pieces.

MIDDLEGAME

The middle phase of a chess game.

OPENING

The phase at the start of a chess game. Can also refer to a tried and tested sequence of moves that allows you to make a good start.

PAWN

The least valuable piece in a chess game. Each player has eight pawns.

QUEEN

The most powerful piece in a chess game. Queens can move as far as they want in any direction. Each player has only one queen.

QUEENSIDE

Refers to the side of the board the queen is on. It is the left side of the board if you're playing as white and the right side of the board if you're playing as black.

RANK

A row (horizontal line) on a chessboard.

ROOK

One of the pieces in a chess game. It can move as far as it wants in straight lines (vertically or horizontally). Each player has two rooks.

SHORT-RANGE PIECE

A chess piece that can't move very many squares in one move. Pawns, knights, and kings are short-range pieces.

WORLD CHESS CHAMPIONSHIP

The tournament that determines the best chess player in the world.

INDEX

This has been a

NEON 🦑 SQUID

production

We've made it! I want to say THANK YOU. I'm so glad you read the book! Now, to get the most out of it, read the book over and over. Repetition is key! I want to dedicate this book to all of my chess friends, followers, fans, supporters, and anyone who consumes my chess content! I get so much joy in knowing that I can help someone get better by watching my content or reading this book. I wish you nothing but success in whatever you do and especially in chess! See ya around, scholar!

Author: James Canty III
Illustrator: Brian Lambert
Consultant: Sarah Longson

Editorial Assistant: Malu Rocha
US Editor: Jill Freshney
Proofreader: Georgina Coles
Indexer: Elizabeth Wise

Copyright © 2024 St. Martin's Press
120 Broadway, New York, NY 10271

Created for St. Martin's Press
by Neon Squid
The Smithson, 6 Briset Street,
London, EC1M 5NR

EU representative: Macmillan
Publishers Ireland Ltd, 1st Floor, The Liffey
Trust Centre, 117–126 Sheriff Street
Upper, Dublin 1, D01 YC43

10 9 8 7 6 5 4 3 2 1

Library of Congress Cataloging-in-Publication Data is available.

Printed and bound in Guangdong, China by Leo Paper Products Ltd.

ISBN: 978-1-684-49387-6

Published in September 2024.

www.neonsquidbooks.com